LENORMAND SPREADS

By the same author:

LES CONTES DES FLEURS SAUVAGES

LE PETIT JEU LENORMAND DÉVOILE ENFIN SON MYSTÈRE, published in 3 volumes:

LENORMAND ASTROLOGIQUE   - Volume 1

TIRAGES LENORMAND   - Volume 2

COMBINAISONS LENORMAND   - Volume 3

THE PETIT JEU LENORMAND FINALLY REVEALS ITS MYSTERY

STELIANA PUJOLRAS

LENORMAND SPREADS

THE PETIT JEU LENORMAND
FINALLY REVEALS ITS MYSTERY

VOLUME 2

ÉDITIONS POST-SCRIPTUM

The Code of intellectual and artistic property allows, under paragraphs 2 and 3 of Article L.122-5, first, that "copies, or reproductions, are strictly reserved for the private use of the copier and not intended for collective use" and, secondly, that "analyzes and short quotations are allowed in purpose of examples, and illustration," so establishes for this work that "any representation or complete or partial reproduction, without the consent of the author, or of his assignee, or of his entitled, inheres unlawful" (paragraph 1 of Article L.122-4). This representation or reproduction, by any means whatsoever, would constitute an infringement punishable under Article L.335-2 and following in the Code of intellectual and artistic property.

The legal depository of the French manuscript *Le Petit Jeu Lenormand dévoile enfin son mystère* has been made to **SNAC** (the National Union of Authors and Composers) in **2013**, **France**. This book represents the second volume of the book *Le Petit Jeu Lenormand finally reveals its mystery*, author Steliana Pujolras. The astrological game cards were made with royalty-free photos and are found entirely in the book mentioned.

Layout and cover: *Steliana Pujolras*

© 2015 Steliana Pujolras, France. All rights reserved.

© 2019 Éditions POST-SCRIPTUM, 63700 Montaigut

Dépôt légal BNF, janvier 2019, France
BNF legal deposit, January 2019, France

Second edition

Print on : **www.amazon.com**

ISBN 979-10-94605-13-4

Man can not perfect himself that by guessing a more perfect order of things.

PIERRE-SIMON BALLANCHE

Foreword

After discovering in the first volume, Astrological Lenormand, the meanings of the Lenormand cards and the astrological signs attributed to each of them by the brilliant creator of the Petit Jeu, the second volume opens the vast field of card draws.

An undeniable fact is obvious: there are as many fortune tellers as methods to draw the cards and vice versa. It was therefore necessary to adapt some draws, which are already classics of traditional cartomancy, to meet the expectations of readers particularly attached to the cards Gentleman and Lady. But it was also necessary to bring a new breath through many new spreads, designed as much for their playful side as for the beauty of the reflection they impose.

Explanations and diagrams as well as a method of calculating the time bring their lighting, to allow the readers an easiest decryption of a domain at the same time fascinating and mysterious.

In this volume, those who are well-informed and beginners will be carried away by the same passion for cartomancy, this unquestionable art that has been chiseled throughout the centuries, with ever brighter and elegance.

SPREADS

Everyone knows in what manner a draw is performed: nothing is easier than shuffle and place the cards. But now, even in basic things, we find specific rules. And especially when we talk about divination cards!

How to be more successful in personal predictions? Simply: by following the tradition and putting a little of his own, because, to read the cards, one must first learn their codes and then bring forth connections. Everyone can do it, on the condition of being persevering in learning and being permeable to suggestions offered by the symbols. The mysteries remain impenetrable only in front of the opacity of the mind; it is enough to accept that other truths can inhere beyond reason or science.

The images printed, as well as the numbers granted to the 36 cards have diverted the decoders' attention from the essential truth, given by the four traditional colors: diamonds, hearts, spades and clubs. Without a manual, this so particular game has allowed all kinds of outlandish theories and the thick mystery surrounding its little quatrains was not deciphered until today.

We discovered in the first volume, Astrological Lenormand, the real meanings of the cards; we must proceed now with the identification of some basic rules of traditional fortune-telling.

For the first analysis of a spread, it will be necessary to retain some ideas:

- The *diamonds* concern the material domain and everything that we do to stabilize our situation (employment, occupations, different actions, businesses, etc.). These cards are generally favorable in a draw, but they depend on heavily on left-right positioning.
- The *hearts* touch the sentimental area and speak as much about love as about friendship or affection. These cards are beneficial.
- The *spades* evoke generally the troubles of the life (sadness, disputes, disappointments, diseases, etc.) These cards are generally unfavorable, with some exceptions.
- The *clubs* represent the financial position, the capital, and the practical side. They are generally favorable.

The explanations given in this book consider the reading of the upright and backwards cards.

From what we know after studying their works, Etteilla and Miss Lenormand were very firm on this point: the backwards cards have the same importance as the cards presented in an upright position. Many fortune tellers believe that backwards cards must be simply interpreted contrary to upright cards, but this is a completely false theory and belied by the fortune-teller tradition that we have studied starting from its roots.

We can therefore establish some general rules for the backward cards, but we must not forget that there are many exceptions in this list that you should learn by heart. As follows:

- ❖ The *reversed diamonds* become less favorable and announce obstacles or confrontations that will delay the promised advantages.
- ❖ The *reversed hearts* lose a part of their beneficial power and let enter the difficulties into the game.
- ❖ The *reversed spades* keep their natural unfavorable sense, with some exceptions.
- ❖ The *reversed clubs* hinder the financial benefits and accentuate the disagreement.

The interpretative process may seem difficult at first, but things improve with the practice. It is not a bad idea to leave the complicated deciphering for later. As soon as the experience settles down, the attention and the understanding pass at an upper level, and the technique is improved.

We can say that there are as many methods to read the cards, as the number of the fortune tellers! To respect a minimum of information is better than paying a comedy of the incantation of the spirits. It will be necessary to start by taking into account the following rules:

- ▪ Mix the deck carefully, and shuffle the cards before each draw. This helps to focus on the question we wish to clear up. Shuffling the cards seven times is a good number. In cartomancy, we use rather the odd numbers as three, seven, eleven, fifteen, twenty-one, etc.

- We cut and put the upper pile underneath the deck of cards. Note the cut; it brings additional indications for the draw. We note first the card which is seen in the upper stack (say X) then the one that is below the deck (say Y) and we read the combination: "*Y near X.*" We place the upper pile underneath so that, at the end of the operation, X is visible under the deck of cards. Some people prefer to cut three times the pile, but a simple cutting is sufficient and more just in the response.

- Note the cards that may fall during these operations, they are also important. If they fall in considerable quantity, if their number is too large, it means that you might obtain an ambiguity in the answers. If you cut too high or too low in the stack (by taking or just leaving a few cards) the result is the same. It is better to stop the draw, because you will not get an honest answer. The cards are clever, they do as they please!

- Do not persist if the response of the cards is unfavorable: we do not obtain the opposite just because we do not want to hear what the cards have to say. In case of an omen very hard to hear, it will be necessary to do the draw three times (for the same question) and not decide the answer before it is confirmed three times. We can thus

obtain a better conclusion and act in the right direction, to soften this prediction and correct the course of events.
- The cards do not work well in too bright places.
- It is not a good idea to lend the personal cards to other people. Many fortune tellers do a mix or cut the cards by their customers but, in this book, we insist on the idea that the cards work better in the hands of their master than in those of a stranger.
- Keep the cards cautiously; they slide better when they are in good condition. They can be "purified" from time to time; the simplest solution is to put them in order. If they are damaged, you can replace them with a new set, but it will be necessary to give them a little time to "get accustomed." Pay attention to their first revelations, as they may turn out to be incorrect.
- Note the draws in a small notebook; it is a remarkable reminder that facilitates the understanding of omens during the days that pass.
- Do not read the cards in the presence of a radio or TV switched on. If certain people read the cards under specific conditions (next to pets or objects that make them happy or reassure them, etc.) it is better to keep this ritual, it will favor an intimate atmosphere beneficial to the concentration.

We must not forget, however, that this is a game created with the purpose of a pastime, such as Etteilla said. It is thus recommended to use it wisely, and not seek the truth of the omens with an exaggerated passion. They only guide the Inquirer, because these images probe the subconscious. The auguries and the personal intuition offer the answers. The Petit Jeu is a wonderful tool of divinatory reflection, but it does not replace the life of every day.

I. CLASSICAL SPREADS

They are classical; we are not going to linger to explain them in detail, just evoke them and allow an overall image of some existing variants to this day. The majority of these variants was adjusted in this book to suit the Petit Jeu, because the order in which the cards are usually spread out by many contemporary fortune tellers (into the Grand Tableau, or in different draws) does not follow the Etteilla and Lenormand traditions. With the exception of two or three draws using a composite arrangement, all the other draws presented in this book respect the fortune teller tradition.

In Lenormand interpreting, the cards are analyzed from the base upward. Similar for Etteilla, who uses (in addition to this!) the analysis from right to left. In many contemporary draws, we often encounter the past at the top and the future towards the base of the assemblage.

Unfortunately, the brilliant creator of the Petit Jeu did not leave us the instructions for use, but we can suppose that he did not distance too much from the traditional way used in cartomancy. Unless he created his own method because, according to what his contemporaries said, Ballanche was "both writer and deep thinker, endowed with a sort of prophetic spirit that made him guess the history and anticipate the theological future."

The procedure is the same for all draws: mix the deck of cards on the table and reshuffle the cards, cut once (left hand, say a lot of fortune tellers, but Etteilla did not mention it), note the two cards of the cutting; now deal the cards as they appear.

Many fortune tellers use the method of picking the cards one by one after shuffling. You can do it if you like it more, but remember that, in this book, we use the traditional method: the cards are drawn as they appear in the game, so one after another. Let us allow the entire honor to the recognized masters of divination games, who considered that the cards combine their secrets according to their own will.

1. THE 3 CARDS SPREAD

| 1 | 2 | 3 |

1 = the past of the Inquirer
2 = the present of the Inquirer
3 = the future of the Inquirer

2. THE 5 CARDS SPREAD

```
      [ 5 ]
[ 2 ][ 3 ][ 4 ]
      [ 1 ]
```

1 = the positive element (favorable to the case)
2 = the negative element (unfavorable to the studied situation)
3 = the arbitrator element (which compares for and against)
4 = the element to be considered (of which the situation depends)
5 = the resolution (which indicates the way of acting)

3. THE 9 CARDS SPREAD

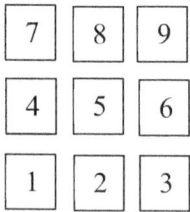

1, 2, 3 = the past of the Inquirer
4, 5, 6 = the present of the Inquirer
7, 8, 9 = the future of the Inquirer

Some people use this draw from left to right:
1, 4, and 7 indicate the past;
2, 5, 8 is the association used for the present and
3, 6, 9 that used for the future.

Both methods are suitable, because the left can be associated with the past (see the explanations in the chapter allocated to the card 28, the Gentleman, in the book *The Petit Jeu Lenormand finally reveals its mystery*).

4. THE GYPSY SPREAD OF 21 CARDS

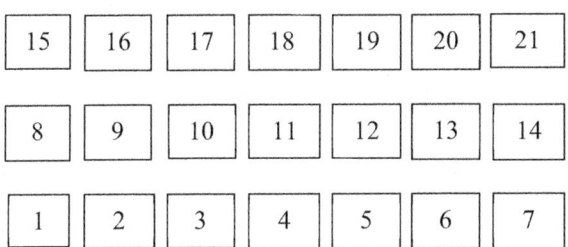

1- 7 = the past of the Inquirer
8–14 = the present of the Inquirer
15–21 = the future of the Inquirer

5. THE HORSESHOE SPREAD OF 21 CARDS

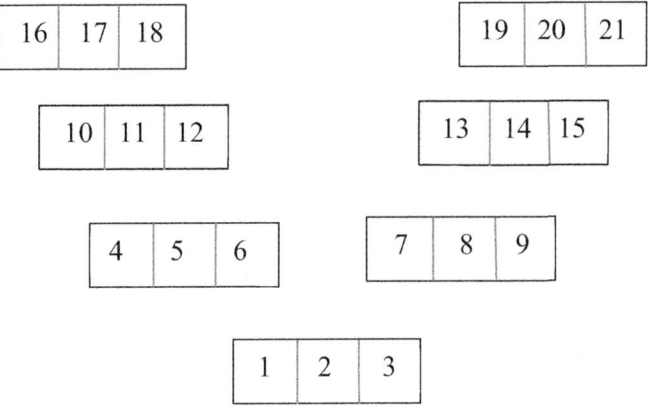

1–3 = the present
4–6 = the problem
7–9 = the obstacles, the oppositions
10–12 = the feelings, the thoughts, the expectations
13–15 = the development of the problem
16–18 = the intentions
19–21 = the future outcome

6. THE SPREAD OF "YES AND NO" QUESTIONS

Here is a very simple, but also very practical draw. It answers questions that we ask about a subject we would like deepen. One could say that it is the draw of "why" and "is it..." Here are the steps to follow:

a) Take out of the pile the card that seems best to summarize the main question. Think of the question and look at this card, in order to visualize it during the draw. Put it back into the package. Mix the cards on the table, then shuffle and make a cut. Note the cut, because it provides additional information for the draw.

b) Put the first card while thinking about the essential question. The card will grant a response which is considered positive (*yes*) or negative (*no*). According to its message, ask another question following the logic of the first question, or the logic of the answer provided by the card.

c) Pull another card that will compel the answer to the previous question and put it underneath the previous card (or close by, it doesn't matter). We continue in the same way until we get to the card that summarizes the main question (the one that was visualized) at the beginning of the game. Once the card went out, the draw stops: it furnished all its answers.

If we wish only a confirmation or advice, we only make a cut, by interpreting the combination. The upper stack turns and shows the card on the left (X), the lower stack shows the card on the right (Y). We read, according to the formula "Y near X" (or "next to," or "close by.") This is the easiest draw possible, but extremely effective.

II. ETTEILLA AND LENORMAND SPREAD

There are very few indications on spreads used by Miss Lenormand. We are not talking about the draws used by Pierre-Simon Ballanche, because nobody has thought of him all this time and his reflections seem lost forever! The fortune tellers and the various authors of books about the Petit Jeu Lenormand use, in their majority, what is called *The Grand Tableau*. This consists in deploying the game of 36 cards from the top down, on 4 lines of 8 cards and a last line (representing the future, according to them) of 4 cards at the bottom of this arrangement, as shown below:

1	2	3	4	5	6	7	8
9	10	11	12	13	14	15	16
17	18	19	20	21	22	23	24
25	26	27	28	29	30	31	32
		33	34	35	36		

We can admit that, from an architectural point of view, this is not the best solution, because the base is unstable and the construction overflows. It is not, indeed, the original composition, but a maximum use of the 36 cards because of a lack of precise information on the Lenormand draw.

As far as we know, Miss Lenormand grew up and lived permanently accompanied by the cards of the game Etteilla. She was thus faithful to their traditional teaching. Although she has enriched, embellished or slightly diverted the direction of some cards for her personal game, she treasured Etteilla's guideline that requires taking out the cards one after another of the pile, to spread or add them like the draw require, from bottom to top.

Everybody remembers a famous lithograph in which we see the Empress Joséphine and Miss Lenormand at Malmaison. The cards that can be seen on the table between the two women are spread in an arc. On the side, we clearly see the cards set apart for the *surprise*, as it was in the customs of the time. This arched arrangement is the one that Etteilla recommended in the beginning of the draws, especially for an Inquirer whom we know little.

We continue with other compositions and, in addition to the traditional draw, we can (with discernment and loyalty to the general rules) invent new draws just as amazing.

7. ETTEILLA'S 12 CARDS SPREAD

This spread is the most faithful to Etteilla tradition. It is the one of which we can be sure that Miss Lenormand has used mostly (in addition to the one that she called *The 25 portrayals' spread*).

It announces 12 cards, but in fact we count 14, because the "surprise" (noted in our example with the letter **S**) is auxiliary. Miss Lenormand used to take away two cards, for the said surprise: one for the "happy unforeseen event," the other for the "unpleasant unforeseen event[1]."

We begin by mixing the cards on the table, then shuffling and cutting. Pull two cards for the surprise by letting them upside down (faces towards the table) until the end of the analysis. Take off as a surprise card the 13th card (that follows so after having disposed the 12 cards in the draw) and the last one in the pile.

The cards are placed in a slight arch in which we seek first the "card of the person" (man or woman Inquirer). From now on we'll call this card "CP," to facilitate the explanations.

In the following schema we place the cards from right to left, as Eteilla had expressly demanded, by loyalty to the Egyptian tradition from which he drew his knowledge.

---

[1] Dimitriadis, Dicta : *Mademoiselle Lenormand voyante de Louis XVI à Louis-*

So, we followed the tradition in the case of this draw, as well as for *The spread in Z* (that develops *The initial draw of 12 cards* of Etteilla, as he used to call it). The other spreads of this book use the numbering from left to right, for the sake of intelligibility and ease of arrangement of cards, according to the conventions of our civilization.

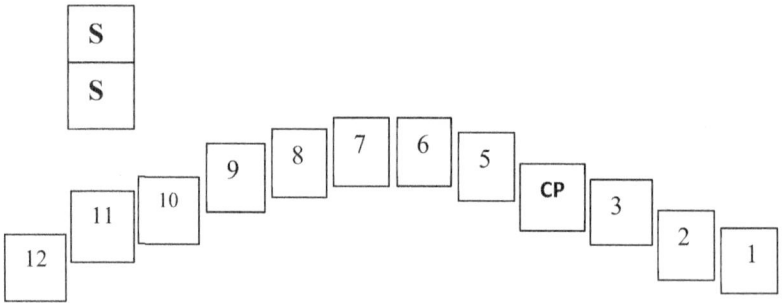

a) We are searching the CP and analyze what is in its vicinity. Generally, if the CP is not getting out, we start again the draw. If the CP is missing the second or third time, we still analyze the cards that are shown up, considering as CP the first card of the row. In this case, Etteilla considered that we are in front of a "passive questioner" (because the CP is not output). For that, the "wise Egyptians" had taught that the Inquirer must be advised to dominate current events in his life and not simply wait their denouement.

b) We are looking for the two, three or four cards that have the same number (e.g., two, three or four cards of Seven: Birds, Letter, Tree, Mice) and which are arranged *in the same direction* (all upright or all reversed). These cards are important in the draw, as they bring forth indications as much alone, as in a combination.

c) We look carefully to see if we find *encounter numbers* in the couples of cards that, added, give the number 31 (e.g., Path and Bouquet: 22 + 9 = 31). These cards cancel each other.

d) We analyze the upright and backwards cards. We analyze the draw a first time, to understand the events that lie ahead. We analyze the cards two by two, from one end to the other: 1 and 12; 2 and 11; 3 and 10 and so on for those who remain.

e) We add the numbers of all twelve cards and, according to Etteilla, the result represents the number of days that close the past, the present and the future of the Inquirer, compared with the information in this draw. More specifically, the information contained in the draw influences twice that number. First, we have the Inquirer's past, for this number of days; secondly, we obtain the future of the Inquirer for the same number of days (for example number **187**: 187 days for the past and 187 days in the future). For details, see the chapter *The calculation of time*.

f) We analyze the draw again, this time for thinking on a higher plane how we can act in the future to anticipate unpleasant events. The course of events can be improved if we draw the right lessons of cards, and if we act accordingly.

8. THE 15 CARDS SPREAD

This is also an Etteilla draw and we thus presume that Miss Lenormand used it too.

You have to spread firstly 5 cards, in order to obtain an answer to the question that interests you. If this answer is vague, add above the first row another 5 cards. You may put still 5 cards if the answer is still not clear, but *no more*!

- Begin by mixing the cards on the table, then shuffle and make a cut.
- Pull two cards for the *surprise* and leave them upside down until the end of the analysis. For that, take out as a surprise card the 16th (that follows so after having distributed 15 cards) and the last one in the pile.
- *Note 1*: If the answers suit you after the first five cards, the surprise cards will be the 6th and the last of the pile.
- *Note 2*: If the answers suit you only after the first ten cards, the surprise cards will be the 11th and the last one in the pile.

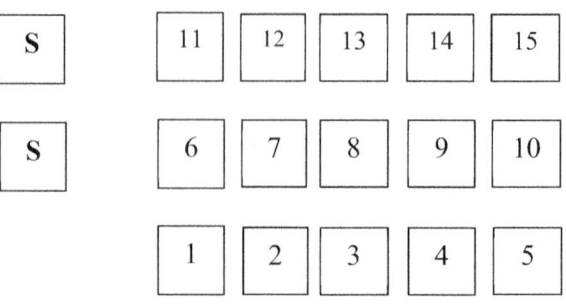

a) We search the CP that has been defined previously, and which has a lot of importance; we analyze what is in its vicinity. We analyze the upright and backwards cards.
b) We analyze the lines of cards according to combinations "Y near X," by not forgetting that rows are broken to the right and that the 6th or 11th card that follows is on the superior row, to the left (6 near 5, 11 near 10, etc.)
c) We look for the groups of two, three or four cards that have the same number (e.g., two, three or four cards of Seven: Birds, Letter, Tree, Mice) and which are arranged in the same direction (all upright or all reversed). These cards are important in the draw because they operate as well alone as in a combination. To have importance in groupings, they must be oriented in the same direction (straight or reversed). The majority decides: for example, if we find two cards of Ten reversed next to a Ten upright, we consider that we are dealing with a trio of Ten reversed.
d) We look attentively to find some *encounter numbers*, thus cards that, added, give the number 31 (e.g., Path and Bouquet: 22 + 9 = 31). This combination is zero, it does not speak. We commence by a first analysis of the draw, in order to understand the responses to the main question.
e) We turn back the cards surprise (one for the "happy unforeseen event," the other for the

"unpleasant unforeseen event") and we analyze the new data in relation with the revelations of the draw.
f) We analyze a second time the spread, in order to think on a higher plane how we can act in the future to improve the course of events. If the answer sought is not given within 15 cards, it means that it will be about a non-success.

This draw was used to answer a specific question and, of what we knew, in that epoch they were also used draws of 7, 13 and 17 cards, which were variants of the 15 cards spread.

Here is an example:

The 7 cards spread:
- *The 1st variant*: spread 5 cards, plus 2 cards representing "the surprise" (one for the "happy unforeseen event," the other for the "unpleasant unforeseen event.") The card surprises are the 6th and the last one below the pile.
- *The 2nd variant*: spread 7 cards in a line, two in the past, and two in the present, two for the future and one for "the surprise." This is also a very good quotidian draw.

LENORMAND SPREADS – *Steliana Pujolras*

9. THE 25 CARDS SPREAD —
or " *Miss Lenormand's 25 portrayals' spread* "

We will now analyze for the first time in a book the draw that we consider to be the real spread Lenormand. We now know today that, unfortunately (except for publications in the newspapers of the time and some books), Alboize du Pujol's family, executor of the Sibyl, destroyed all the correspondence and manuscripts of Miss Lenormand after the death of this one.

Over the years, very few authors explored the information on the famous prophetess's life. *The 25 portrayals' spread* has never been reconsidered in this way, perhaps because nobody observed an obvious link with the game of 36 cards. So, here is this famous draw in a quasi-unexpected (but so perfect!) form of a square of 5 x 5:

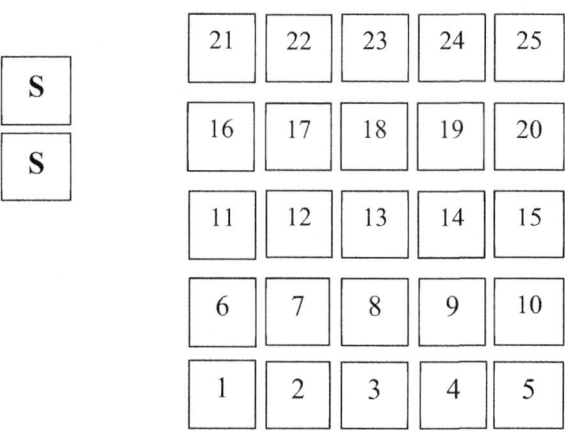

It seems that Miss Lenormand was very devoted to this draw (we found a brief mention in a historical document) as well as to the draws of 7, 13 or 17 cards.

Compared to these three last ones, the draw of *25 portrayals* was intended to provide an ampler image of the Inquirer's life at a certain time. Its name refers to 25 cards, but do not forget that Miss Lenormand was faithful to the tradition that requires bringing out in the game the two cards surprises.

Here now some considerations of mathematical order that don't affect the spreads. The comments below are too stringent, you may *not take them into account* more than just brief remarks or curiosities.

- As we can notice it, this draw is well balanced and the 13th game card is equidistant from all edges and corners of the diagram.
- This arrangement allows us to draw a perfect cross, with the arms 11-12-13-14-15 and 3-8-13-18–23, where the sum of the numbers gives 65 for each arm. Moreover, this cross will be found later in another draw, entitled *The Cross of time*.
- The other perfect Cross is that given by the intersection of diagonals 5-9-13-17–21 and 1-7-13-19–25; the addition of these numbers also gives the result of 65 for each arm.
- Look at the two crosses: that of the center and the one lying diagonally. For each of them, the intersection point is the number 13 cards.

- On all four arms, in adding the numbers to the left and to the right of the card 13, they give 26 each time (twice the central card 13). We obtain the number 26 eight times in the arms of these two crosses.
- Now look at the groups of 4 cards in the corners of the table and bounded by this central cross. You will notice that the two numbers added on the diagonals of each group give the same result. For the group (16–22, 17–21) the result is every time 38. For the group (19–25, 20–24) the result is every time 44. For the group (1–7, 2–6) the result is every time 8. For the group (4–10, 5–9) the result is every time 14.
- If we compare these four groups of cards, the results obtained previously for small diagonals combine themselves, similarly, in the opposed groups. The diagonal of the left group at the top plus the diagonal of the right-low group give us: 38 + 14 = 52. The diagonal of the group that is situated right-up, plus the diagonal of the left-lower group: 44 + 8 = 52.
- We can next continue with the squares of nine cards that are inside this table and that organize themselves on mathematical rules; but we stop here, because " what had to be proven ... is proven!" The mathematical associations will not be absolutely necessary because they will complicate too much the analysis. But for readers who want an even greater approach of the secrets of their

spreads, these associations may be taken into account.

This draw is of an impeccable equilibrium, and its layout is absolutely wonderful. Let's see *the main rules* of this draw:

a) Mix the cards on the table, then shuffle and make a cut. The spread is deployed completely, with all the cards presented as they come out of the stack, upright or reversed. We look where the CP is and we analyze its neighborhood. We analyze the cards (upright and reversed).

b) If the CP is positioned in a corner of the table, the Inquirer is at a crossroads in his life and a major event upsets him (or her). If the CP is positioned in the center, the Inquirer is able to control his life, but he is in the middle of events. The CP is, generally, one of the figures of the game. Choose it by following the peculiar features of the cards, or simply according to the intuition of the Inquirer.

c) We identify the Kings, the Queens and the Jacks by human figures and, thus, by people known by the Inquirer.

d) We look for the groups of two, three or four cards that have the same number (e.g., two, three or four cards of Seven: Birds, Letter, Tree, Mice) and which are spread in the same direction (all upright or reversed). These cards are important in the draw because they operate as well alone as in groups. To have significance in a grouping, they must be oriented in the same direction (upright or backwards cards).

e) We look attentively trying to find any encounter numbers, thus cards which, added, give us the number 31 (e.g., Path and Bouquet: 22 + 9 = 31). Etteilla has called this subtotal an "encounter number" and considered this as null association.

f) We analyze for a first time the spread (upright and backwards cards) to understand the main information that stands out. The reading goes from left to right and from bottom to top for the chronology. You can also complete the interpretation by groups of cards and according to the personal inspiration.

g) We analyze the present of the Inquirer on the line on which is situated the CP. The CP is situated in the present of the Inquirer, because the CP is the Inquirer. Cards that are on the left and right of the CP represent the closest moments of the past and future. What lies below the line that contains the CP belongs to the past of the Inquirer. What lies above the line that contains the CP concerns the future of the Inquirer.

h) If the CP card is positioned exactly in the center of the draw, we analyze the present of the Inquirer on the central cross, vertically and horizontally, thus on the arms (11-12-13-14-15) and (3-8-13-18–23).

i) We return the two cards surprise (one for the "happy unforeseen event," the other one for the "unpleasant unforeseen event") and we analyze the new data in relation with the revelations of the draw.

Supplement: We will now add some special remarks *only* for the Inquirers who consider the Lady or the Gentleman as being the cards of the person (CP).

As one can easily observe, the principle of contrary (that attract themselves, however!) is respected once again: the Lady and the Gentleman look towards opposite directions. The Gentleman's face (card 28) is turned to the right, while the Lady (card 29) looks towards the left. These two Aces are an innovation in the Petit Jeu, because Pierre-Simon Ballanche had needed a distinctive representation of the two principles (male and female) in his allegory. The traditional cards do not have human figures for the Aces, but only for the Kings, Queens and the Jacks. Etteilla himself had only a single card for the Inquirer or the "questioner," as he called him.

Some Petits Jeux were drawn thereafter with two characters (Gentleman and Lady) looking straight ahead, to facilitate the interpretation. But the opposite glance of the characters can bring more pungent information, according to the contemporary fortune telling. If we consider these two cards as being the CPs, both CP back-to-back would mean that the Gentleman and the Lady ignore each other, while in inverse position they are looking each other in life. This is additional information for the charm of the game, and we can so analyze what lies between the two cards 28 and 29 as follows:

- For the situation in which the card 28 is at the top of the draw, the two characters have the back turned one to another. The past is in their back, it means that it doesn't exist much commitment between them at the moment. We could possibly find the explanations in the cards that separate them.

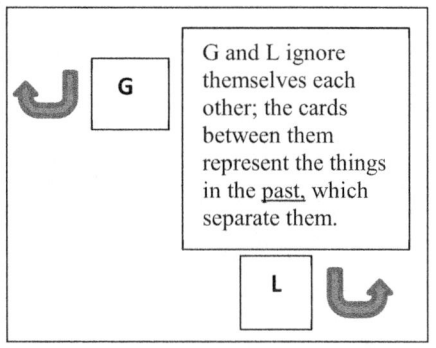

> G and L ignore themselves each other; the cards between them represent the things in the past, which separate them.

- For the situation in which the card 29 is on top of the draw, both characters look each other. Their future being among them, this means that there are feelings or things to be shared. The cards, positioned between the cards 29 and 28, offer indications onto the nature of these exchanges.

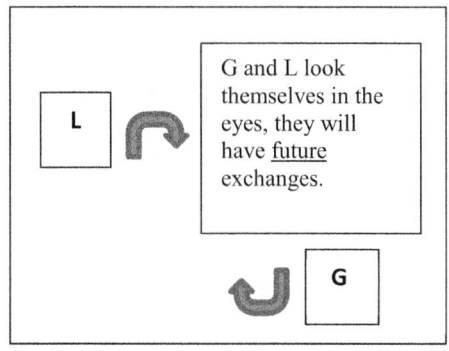

> G and L look themselves in the eyes, they will have future exchanges.

- For the situation in which the CP appears without its "half," we deduce that the partner does not own an important role in Inquirer's life, for this distinctive draw.

Once again: the visual interpretation is a poetical analysis, imagined in this book for the pleasure of the eyes and the comfort of the readers who feel particularly attached to these two characters! This kind of interpretation will be a personal choice (that is not in agreement with the fortune-teller tradition). It will then be necessary to take into account that the combination of various Aces can distort the omens (for example: three Aces together in a draw announce difficulties, four Aces announce the triumph).

III. SPREADS DERIVED FROM LENORMAND DISPOSITION

10. THE GRAND TABLEAU

		33	34	35	36		
25	26	27	28	29	30	31	32
17	18	19	20	21	22	23	24
9	10	11	12	13	14	15	16
1	2	3	4	5	6	7	8

To date, *The Grand Tableau* is the most popular draw among the followers of the Petit Jeu Lenormand.

In a concern of loyalty for all the cards, but also by lack of information on the original draw, the cards were used in this arrangement. This accedes to the impression of having access to all the secrets of the life of the Inquirer.

Thus, the cards are moved away of their function of sovereign oracle and forced to display their secrets to the command, as in an inventory. The cards do not work thus. They can sometimes be stubborn, sometimes malicious, but always clever! Do not forget that we address them with a sense of subordination and dependency, which reinforces them in the influence that they have on the Inquirer. The answers they give are not necessarily the ones that are expected, or those that we command.

In this form, *The Grand Tableau* of 36 cards may be seen rather as an enlarged use of *The 25 Portrayals' Spread*, even if it doesn't provide a more powerful omen that the original matrix of 25 cards. The 36 cards are combined in such a wonderful way in *The Astrological Spread*, which holds of the genius creator of the writer philosopher Pierre-Simon Ballanche.

In this book, *The Grand Tableau* is presented with four cards on the top. As already explained, we believe that the top of the diagram represents the future, so the outcome, the solution or resolution of the draw, which is so contained in a limited number of cards.

As a general rule in the diagrams in this book, the past is at the basis, the future at the top. This structure is made taking into account that the cards, which overlay the previous card, influence it and, quite often, determine it. As rules of reading, we take what has already been stated in *The 25 Portrayals' Spread*.

11. THE MOREAU SPREAD

This spread is reproduced according to Adèle Moreau's indications, who claimed herself "student of Miss Lenormand" as dozens of others who succeeded her, and it was recorded in a book[*].

Like all other Lenormand spreads, it appears "upside down" (the three cards of the future are at the bottom). We allowed ourselves to reverse it (but also to adjust its indications) so that it adapts itself to the explanations in this book.

This is an arrangement of 24 cards, plus the CP, which you get out of the stack before shuffling, but is also an interpretation according to the sighting of the Lady or the Gentleman.

Here are the rules of the Moreau spread:
a) We choose the CP according to the Inquirer; we mix the cards on the table, then shuffle and cut.
b) We unfold a line of 7 cards at the bottom of the diagram, and the eighth at the top, to the left, at an interval of two rows.
c) We continue with a second line of 7, and the eighth card (number 16 in the pile) is placed at the top, next to the first one.
d) We align finally the third line of 7, and the eighth card (number 24 in the stack) joins the other two at the top of the arrangement.

---

[*]Dos Ventos, Mario : *The Game of Destiny, Fortune Telling with Lenormand Cards*

e) We put the CP on the card number 12 of the spread. We analyze while taking into account in this draw of the direction in which the CP watches, knowing that the back of the character is turned towards the past.

CP					
		8	16	24	
17	18	19	20	21	22	23
9	10	11	12/ CP	13	14	15
1	2	3	4	5	6	7

The Moreau spread stops here the indications. We obtain no explanation for the group of three cards 8-16-24, or for chronology. The author says that the direction of CP's gazes indicates the future and what is in the back of the characters is the past. But the images of these two characters in his book are oriented the same way, the Lady and the Gentleman are drawn seen from the front and it is not obvious in which direction they look. So let's go further in the deduction, to arrive at an explanation for the Petit Jeu edited by Cartamundi. Thus:

- If the CP is the card 28 (the Gentleman, who looks to his right and therefore towards the future): his past is into his back and therefore in the group (1-2-3-4-5-6-7-13-14-15); his future is in the group (9-10-11-17-18-19-20-21-22-23-8-16-24), where (8-16-24) represent the cards surprise.
- If the CP is the card 29 (the Lady, who looks to her left and therefore towards the past): her past is in the group (1-2-3-4-5-6-7-13-14 -15); her future is in the groups (9-10-11-17-18-19-20-21-22-23) and (8-16-24).

In both cases, the past is bottom and the future upward. So we find no difference between the two cards based on the look, which comforts Etteilla's theory that we can choose any game card to represent the CP.

One might suspect Adele Moreau of having wanted to create a synonym of *The 25 portrayals' spread*, without refining its method. Or, nevertheless, we can eventually think that she has not provided enough information to her disciples, to those who have resumed the Moreau spread afterward. As Etteilla had given free hand to the "deployment of twelve, twenty-one, or any other number, at the free will of the fortune teller or the Inquirer[*2]," we can, however, understand that each performer tries to create his own rule.

---

[*] Etteilla: *L'astrologie du livre de Thot*, page 254
[**] Dos Ventos, Mario: *The Game of Destiny, Fortune Telling with Lenormand Cards*

It is true that Miss Lenormand's *25 portrayals' spread* might lead to a confusion with *The Moreau spread of 25 cards*. We know that Miss Lenormand did not leave behind her any drafts for her spreads, but it will be necessary to remember that she always sought the perfection of her actions and methods. She would in no way abdicated of the tradition that imposed to always draw surprise cards. Thus, *The 25 portrayals' spread* counted a few more cards than Adele Moreau has left for her own arrangement.

This draw was presented only with respect of a duty of memory, but we do not approve the past-future interpretation depending on the gazes[**] of the characters. We are faithful to the principle that all cards arrange themselves in order: the past downward, and the future upward. The gaze of the characters refers primarily to the indication "right—left," to differentiate the man right side (involving actions) of the left feminine side (that of contemplation and rest).

12. THE SPREAD IN THREE DIMENSIONS

This is a very interesting draw, but more complicated for a beginner. It consists in spreading the cards as though for the *Grand Tableau* and then visualizing a combination of adjacent cards, not only among themselves, but also with the entire set of 36 cards. We thus have the 36 cards in front of us. Each card in the first line is analyzed in relation to its neighbor, but also with the number 1 card, number 2, number 3, etc. of the Petit Jeu.

Example: Suppose the first row of the *Grand Tableau* formed by the cards: 4, 15, 32, 7, 33, 11, 10, and 9.

- We analyze: 4 with 15, and 4 with **1**. (We keep the traditional analysis: *15 near 4*.)
- Then: 15 with 32 (we say *32 near 15*) and 15 with **2**.
- Then: 32 with 7 (*7 near 32*) and 32 with **3**, etc.
- We maintain order until the end of the game, so up to the card **36**.

IV. NEW SPREADS

Let's continue this exploration into the captivating parade of spreads with some novel examples, which are the result of personal reflections of the author in this book. You can always invent new spreads if you consider, of course, some basic rules, as they have been exposed so far. Let us begin with the simplest draw, which can be used daily. Then we will progress by increasing the number of participating cards.

13. THE ENCOUNTER QUESTIONS' SPREAD

This draw develops *The Yes and No* spread that was explained previously. It retakes almost the same technique, but in a slightly more sophisticated way. Instead of taking one card from the stack for each question, we pull two: one above and one below the pile, for each question.

a) We pick up of the packet the card that seems best to summarize the main issue. We think to this question and look at the card, to be able to visualize it, during the draw. Then we pose this card back into the pile.vMix the cards faces to the table, then shuffle and cut. Note the cutting, because it brings additional information into the draw.

b) We lay the first two cards while thinking about the question. The combination of cards will beget a response which is considered positive (*yes*) or negative (*no*). According to this message we'll ask another question, following the logic of the first one.

c) We take two other cards (above and below the pile) that give the answer to the previous question and we pose them on the table. This continues until we get to the card that summarizes the main question, therefore, one that has been visualized at the beginning of the game. Once this card is found, the draw stops.

d) We are searching for the pairs of cards owning the same value and which are displayed in the same direction (upright or reversed). The cards that are on and underneath the pile form a pair. For they matter in combination of pairs, the two cards must be pulled together and be oriented in the same direction (upright or reversed). We analyze the answer given by these cards.

e) We look attentively, to find encounter numbers, meaning pairs of cards that added together give the number 31 (e.g., Path and Bouquet: 22 + 9 = 31). Their answer is no, we do not take it into account.

f) We take into account the backwards cards when we analyze the answer of a pair.

14. THE PYRAMIDAL SPREAD
—a daily 7 card spread

This is a small draw that may be presented in two variants, one as accessible and interesting as the other:

a) **The variant " past—present—future ":**

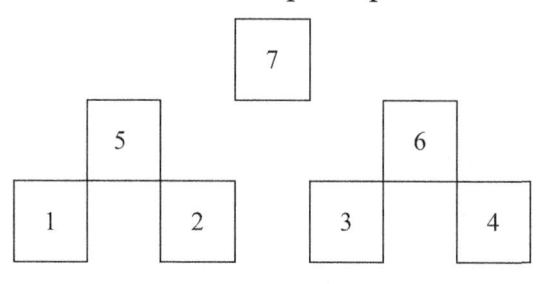

```
              ┌───┐
              │ 7 │
      ┌───┐   └───┘   ┌───┐
      │ 5 │           │ 6 │
┌───┐ └───┘ ┌───┐ ┌───┐ └───┘ ┌───┐
│ 1 │   │ 2 │ │ 3 │   │ 4 │
└───┘   └───┘ └───┘   └───┘
```

1–2—5 = the past (yesterday)
3–4—6 = the present (today)
5–6—7 = the future (tomorrow)

The spread here is surprising because the past is on the left and not down, while the present is to the right and not on the horizontal median line. But we have seen in this book that the left is also an evocation of the past. This arrangement thus combines in a subtle way the three divisions of time, by highlighting, in each one, the influences of the one that precedes it.

b) **The variant "problem—solution":**
Keep the same pattern as in the variant a):
1–2—3-4   = the problem
5–6   = the evolution of the problem
7   = the solution

15. THE DIAMOND SPREAD

The next spread is useful when we want to analyze the causes and the course of prolonged trouble. Take out the CP of the stack and mix slightly, then reshuffle and cut the cards. 12 cards are spread in a spiral conducted according to the Egyptian tradition, from right to left. The 13th card is added to the CP at the end of the interpretation, because it shows the solution to this disagreement.

In this draw, all added cards (1 + 2 + 3 + ... 13) give the number 78 as the total sum. This is the number of the famous pages of the *Book of Thoth* which, according to Etteilla, contained the Science of Universe.

		10		
	5	1	6	
9	4	CP/13	2	11
	8	3	7	
		12		

- CP = card of the person (of the Inquirer)
- 8—3–7—12   = the past
- 9–4—CP — 2–11 = the present
- 5—1–6—10   = the future
- 12   = the origin of the problem
- 8–7 = what has been acquired and remains unchangeable
- 3   = the attitude of the Inquirer in front of his problem
- 9–4 = the current problem and the cause of its return
- 2–11= the solution envisaged for this problem
- 5–6 = the feelings, worries and expectations of the Inquirer
- 1   = the hidden desire of the Inquirer
- 10   = the reason susceptible to modify the future
- 13   = central card of the draw, it shows on what depends the solution of the problem; arises on the CP, at the end of the reading.

16. THE SMALL LOOP SPREAD

In *The Small Loop*, the placing of the cards is also done in a spiral, as in the previous spread. This draw is very interesting for the analysis of a situation.

The past, present and future converge on a line, in harmoniously intertwining. We perceive a connecting link between them: each of these periods has its roots in the period before it, and the peak in the period that follows.

a) Choose in the stack of 36 cards the one that summarizes the problem and keep it. Mix the cards face on the table, then shuffle the rest of cards and cut them. Put in position 1 the card that you selected at the beginning.
b) Lay out the cards by small groups, in the order of the pile, by beginning with the past, then continuing with the present and the future.
c) Analyze the draw by looking at the concentration of the colors (diamonds, hearts, etc.) and the combinations of the nearby cards, by two or by three. Take into account backwards cards and pairs.

LENORMAND SPREADS – *Steliana Pujolras*

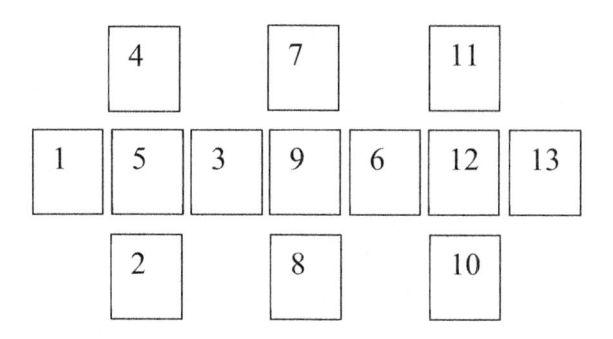

```
        [ 4 ]         [ 7 ]          [ 11 ]
[ 1 ][ 5 ][ 3 ][ 9 ][ 6 ][ 12 ][ 13 ]
        [ 2 ]         [ 8 ]          [ 10 ]
```

- 1–2–3–4–5   = the past
- 3–6—7–8—9   = the present
- 6–10—11–12—13   = the future
- 1–5—3–9—6–12—13   = the evolution of the situation
- 1   = the problem
- 3   = what connects the past to the present
- 6   = what connects the present to the future
- 13   = the outcome of the problem
- 2–8—10   = what is already acquired and cannot be changed
- 4–7—11   = his or her feelings and thoughts on the progress of the situation

17. THE BIG LOOP SPREAD

The Big Loop is a more elaborated form of *The Diamond Spread* and *The Small Loop,* because the analysis includes the alignment of the 12 Houses of the Astrological Wheel.

The emplacement of the cards is always done in a spiral. What is remarkable is the fact that the sum of the 12 cards that compose the Astrological Wheel is 144, so twelve times twelve.

The past, present and future are linked together once again to horizontal, in a harmonious interlacing. We divine a connecting link between them; each of these periods has its roots in the earlier period and the tip in the period that follows.

This kind of arrangement is not possible with more cards. It is necessary to limit the cards number, in order to balance their reciprocal influences, but also for not to be forced to analyze large groups, superior to four cards.

This pattern looks complicated, but it is only an impression. Once this draw is deployed, we easily understand its logic.

a) Choose in the package of 36 cards the one that summarizes the problem and keep it. Mix the cards faces to the table, then shuffle and cut. Place in position **1** the card selected at the beginning.
b) Spread the cards by small groups, in the order of the stack, beginning with the past, and then continuing with the present and the future.

c) Analyze the draw by looking at the concentration of colors (diamonds, hearts, etc.) and the combinations of the adjacent cards by two or by three. Take into account backwards cards and the groupings.
d) For those who wish, the analysis continues with the Astrological Wheel, according the manner of astrologers, considering the Houses 1 to 12. These Houses are on the loop formed by the locations of cards: 18, 15, 4, 5, 2, 16, 20, 17, 10, 12, 11, and 14.

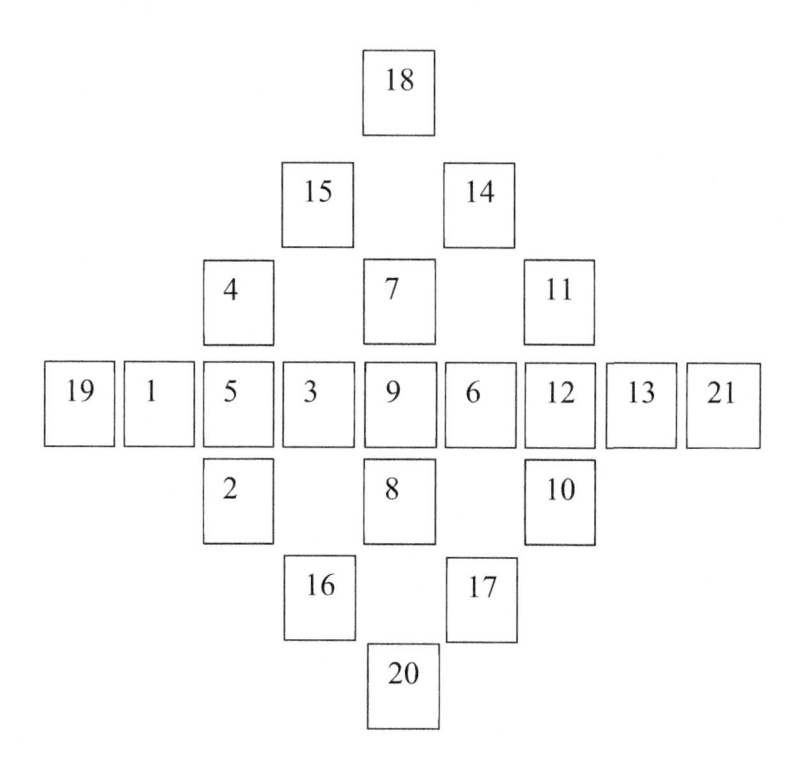

			18					
		15		14				
	4		7		11			
19	1	5	3	9	6	12	13	21
		2		8		10		
		16		17				
			20					

- 19-1-2—3-4—5   = the past
- 3-6—7-8—9   = the present
- 6-10—11-12—13-21   = the future
- 1-5—3-9—6-12—13   = the evolution of the situation
- 1   = the problem
- 3   = whatever links the past to the present;
- 6   = whatever links the present to the future
- 13   = the solution of the problem
- 2-8—10   = what is already acquired and cannot be changed
- 16-17   = the reality
- 20   = the unforeseen that can intervene or change the current condition of the problem
- 4-7—11   = the feelings, fears and expectations of the Inquirer
- 14-15   = the hopes or the hidden desire of the Inquirer
- 18   = the heart's advice
- 19   = explanation on the origin or cause of the problem
- 21   = the future (or the future solution)

18. THE GREAT PYRAMID SPREAD

After the pyramidal spread of 7 cards, now see how we can amplify the teachings that this type of construction can offer.

The Great Pyramid is a draw of reflection in an obsessing concern. It is maybe less complex than *The Big Loop*, but just as effective.

This is a draw that you can remember and visualize with ease even after having arranged the cards in their box. The draw allows later reflections and thus to find additional answers to the annoyance that is in question.

Apart from the admiration for its aesthetics and its famous form, in this kind of arrangement we find the crux of the problem within the pyramid and the key at the top.

a) Choose the CP or the card that, according to the Inquirer, describes best the problem.
b) Mix the cards face on the table, then shuffle and cut. Note the cutting.
c) Spread the cards and place, in the 3rd position, the card selected at the beginning.
d) The draw is interpreted as it was taught up to here.

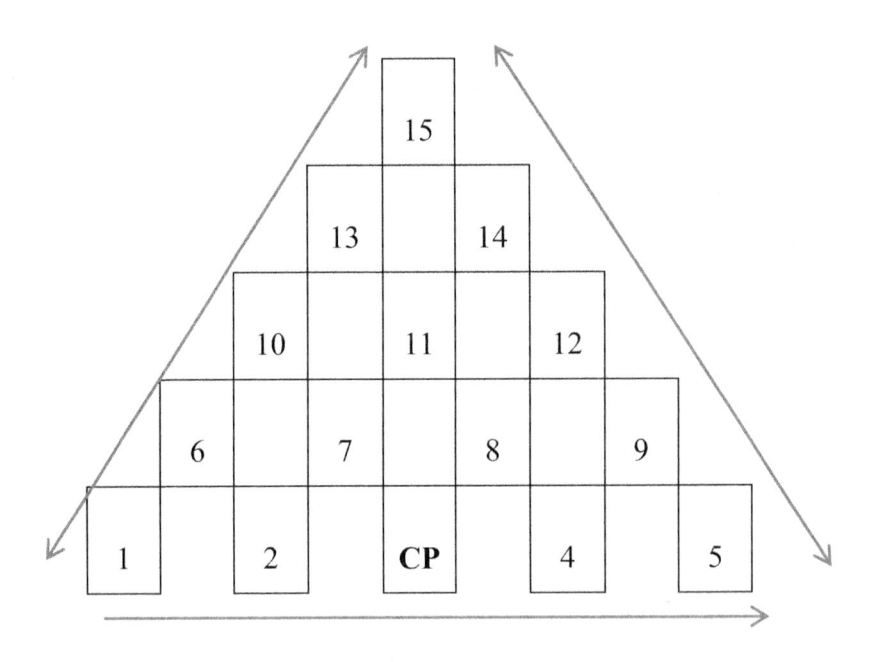

- 1–2–CP–4–5 = the problem
- 1–6–10–13 = what was acquired
- 5–9–12–14 = what is underway
- CP–2–7–11-8-4 = the crux of the problem
- 7–8–11 = the expectations and hopes of the Inquirer
- 15 = the key of the problem

19. THE HEART'S SPREAD

Now, for the pleasure of the eyes, let's see a lovely spread which, despite its small size, has everything to become a favorite draw. It uses the right number of cards, also two CP (Lady and Gentleman). It is easy to remember and, icing on the cake, it protects the sentimental life of the Inquirer.

Heart's spread of **13 cards:**

a) Take out of the game the two CP cards, mix them face to table and let them aside, still facing the table. Shuffle and cut the stack, note the cutting.
b) Arrange the cards face towards the table and be attentive to position the two previously mixed CP (no matter how they present themselves, upright or reversed) before spreading the rest of 11 cards. Turn cards progressively. We interpret the draw as it was taught.

```
         ┌────┐
         │ 11 │
    ┌────┼────┼────┐
    │  8 │  9 │ 10 │
┌───┼────┼────┼────┼───┐
│ 5 │ CP │  6 │ CP │ 7 │
└───┼────┼────┼────┼───┘
    │  2 │  3 │  4 │
    └────┼────┼────┘
         │  1 │
         └────┘
```

- 1   = the basis of the relationship
- 2–3—4   = the past actions that led to the current situation
- 5—CP — 6—CP—7   = the feelings in the present
- 8–9—10   = the thoughts on the reality
- 3–6—9   = what unites or separates the two CPs
- 3   = the element that caused the current situation
- 9   = the thought, common to both CPs
- 6   = what have in common the two CPs
- 11   = the future of the relationship

Heart's spread of **15 cards**:

a) Take out of the game the two CP cards, mix them face to table and let them aside, still facing the table.
b) Shuffle and cut the stack, note the cutting.
c) Arrange the cards face towards the table and position the two previously mixed CP (no matter how they present themselves, upright or reversed) before spreading the rest of 13 cards.
d) Turn cards progressively. We interpret the draw as it was taught up to here.
e) We notice that the number 78 (that encloses, according to Etteilla, the whole science of the Universe) is found in the addition of all the diagram's edges, while the 13th is placed between both CPs.

4	10	5	11	6
9	CP	13	CP	12
3	8	2	7	1

- 3–8 — 2–7 - 1   = the past actions that led to the current situation
- 9 — CP — 13 — CP — 12 = the feelings in the present
- 4–10 — 5–11 — 6   = the future of the relationship
- 2–13 — 5   = what unites or separates the two CP
- 2   = the element that caused the current situation
- 13   = what both CPs cards have in common
- 5   = the common thought of both CP
- 4–10 — 5   = the thoughts of the first CP about the relationship
- 5–11 — 6   = the thoughts of the second CP about the relationship

20. THE SPREAD IN Z

The spread in Z is a variant developed by using Etteilla's *Initial draw of 12 cards*. It allows full use of the 36 cards of the Petit Jeu Lenormand and offers a linear reading, easier to follow.

After shuffling and cutting, we interpret the cards by pairs of two, following the rule suggested by Etteilla, who counsels reading from right to left. Both geometric angles are important for the reading; they are not unimportant because they contain key information.

The time for the predictions applies as in *The calculation of time*, and it is the same for the other spreads.

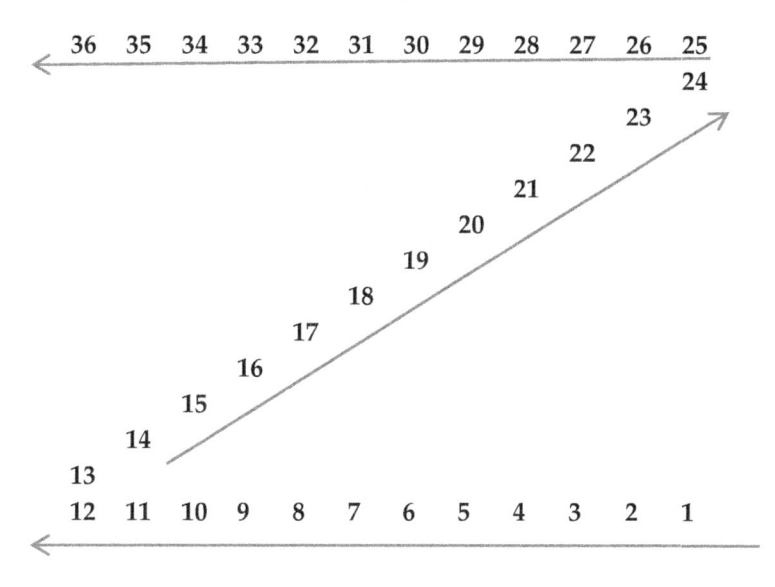

```
← 36  35  34  33  32  31  30  29  28  27  26  25
                                              24
                                          23
                                      22
                                  21
                              20
                          19
                      18
                  17
              16
          15
      14
  13
  12  11  10  9   8   7   6   5   4   3   2   1
←
```

This zigzag is pertinent. It allows focus on the cards linking, more than in usual spreads of 36 cards (where the linking is cut at the end of each row). It respects all the rules imposed by Etteilla.

It allows joining the cards in a single line (divided by two articulations, allowing arrange all the cards on an ordinary table).

It allows the calculation of time after Etteilla's method. Also, the ratio between the numbers brings a particular touch. The arithmetic magic operates here, as in other classifications present in this work. Let's look the three lines of this **Z** (noted by: a, b, and c) after it was bent:

a:	36	35	34	33	32	31	30	29	28	27	26	25
b:	13	14	15	16	17	18	19	20	21	22	23	24
c:	12	11	10	9	8	7	6	5	4	3	2	1

If we add up the columns of the two lines (**a + b**) and use the recursive reduction, we obtain the same sum for each of twelve columns, the **4**.

Similarly, for (**b + c**) we obtain every time the number 25 (that, after the recursive reduction, gives the number **7** in every column).

a:	36	35	34	33	32	31	30	29	28	27	26	25
b:	13	14	15	16	17	18	19	20	21	22	23	24
c:	12	11	10	9	8	7	6	5	4	3	2	1
a+b	49	49	49	49	49	49	49	49	49	49	49	49
	4+9 = 13	…	…	…	…	…	…	…	…	…	…	…
	13 = 1+3 = 4	4	4	4	4	4	4	4	4	4	4	4
b+c	25 = 2+5 = 7	7	7	7	7	7	7	7	7	7	7	7

Also, in the same table, by adding up the columns leads to a repetitive series:

a:	36	35	34	33	32	31	30	29	28	27	26	25
b:	13	14	15	16	17	18	19	20	21	22	23	24
c:	12	11	10	9	8	7	6	5	4	3	2	1
a+b +c:	61	60	59	58	57	56	55	54	53	52	51	50
so:	6+1 = 7	6+0 = 6	5+9 = 14 1+4 = 5	5+8 = 13 1+3 = 4	…	…	…	…	…	…	…	…
a+b +c:	7	6	5	4	3	2	1	9	8	7	6	5

The sum of columns placed in a position of "mirror" in this table (on the last line, from the ends towards the center) always ends with the number **3**: 7+5 = 12 = **3**; 6+6 = 12 = **3**; 5+7 = 12 = **3**; 4+8 = 12 = **3**; 3+9 = 12 = **3**; 2+1 = **3**.

Following the indications of Etteilla (who used to analyze the cards by pairs) starting from the extremities and then applying the recursive reduction, the same amount is obtained for each pair of this spread in Z: 1+ 36 = **37**;   2 + 35 = **37**;   3 + 34 = **37**, etc. (Where, for 37 we have: 3 + 7 = 10, then 1 + 0 = **1**, the first number, *the unit* each time.)

We might continue with the other combinations, because the possibilities of composition are numerous, but arithmetical fantasy is not the purpose of this work. What it will be necessary to retain, is that the attraction of numbers is powerful; it influences the cards and is offering, in the Petit Jeu, an unexpected point of view.

21. THE CROSS OF TIME

Spread recommended when we wish to take stock of the Inquirer's life by analyzing his (or her) past actions, the present and the future, by putting the whole in a relation of interdependence. The name of this draw already exists in the applications of the fortune-telling, but it is classified in the chapter of the new spreads because of the completely inventive way with which it is approached in this book.

The Cross of Time does not have the same theme of study as *The Grand Tableau,* which is especially used to picture the life of the Inquirer at the specific moment of the draw.

S /36	29	30	31	10	32	33	34
	23	24	25	9	26	27	28
	3	4	5	**CP** /36	6	7	8
	17	18	19	2	20	21	22
	11	12	13	1	14	15	16

a) Take out of the game the CP and let it aside on the table. Mix the cards face to table, then shuffle and cut the stack. Note the cutting.

b) Arrange the cards face towards the table and position the CP that was chosen, before spreading the rest of 34 cards.
c) The last card of the pack (the 36th) arises next to the spread or on the CP, at the end of the analysis. This is the card-**Surprise**, the unforeseen element.
d) Turn the cards by groups of six, by analyzing them progressively. You obtain two groups of six cards for the past, and two groups for the future. The two arms of the cross are analyzed for the present.
e) Interpret the draw as it was learned up to here.

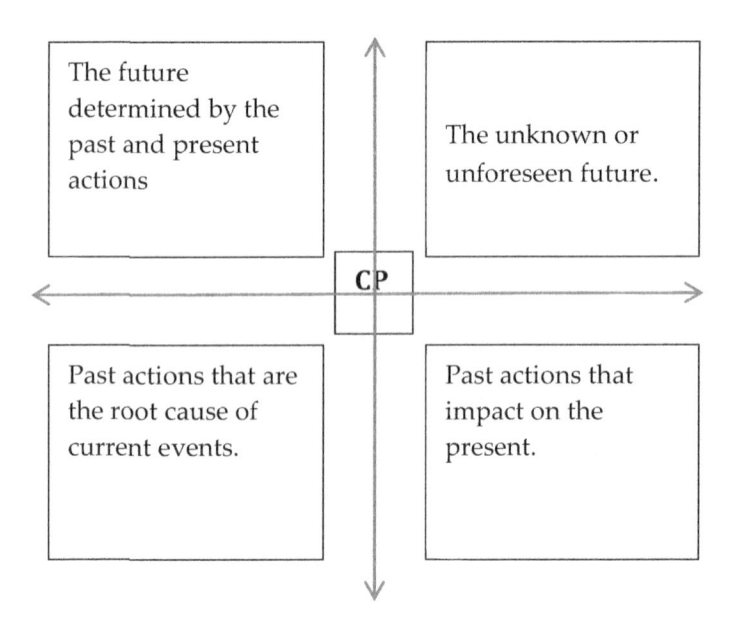

The future determined by the past and present actions	The unknown or unforeseen future.
CP	
Past actions that are the root cause of current events.	Past actions that impact on the present.

- 1–2—CP— 9–10   = the present
- 3–4—5—CP — 6–7—8   = the present
- 11–12—13–17—18–19   = the past actions which are the root cause of the current events
- 14–15—16–20—21–22   = the past actions which impact on the present
- 23–24—25–29—30–31   = the future determined by the actions of the past and present
- 26–27—28–32—33–34   = the unknown or unforeseen future.

22. THE ASTROLOGICAL SPREAD —

predictions for a year:

This spread refers to the ASTROLOGICAL TABLE BALLANCHE, which can be found in the chapter named alike. This draw provides predictions for a year. It can be used either to get an image of the Inquirer's life at a particular moment of the year, or for a question needing a complex answer, which will be spread over twelve months.

The principle is to analyze not only the 36 cards of the spread, but also the pairs of cards that will be in the same table cell. These cells are either the real ones (that the cards will occupy after their distribution in the table) or the virtual ones (attributed automatically, or by default, by the ASTROLOGICAL TABLE BALLANCHE). All must respect the rules indicated in this book (meaning of upright or backwards cards, groups of cards of equal value, etc.).

This will provide an analysis for every month of the year. Each astrological sign will have its own pair of two cards, to study them together, besides the study of the arrangement of 36 cards in the draw.

a) Mix the cards face on the table, then shuffle and cut. Note the cutting: this is a supplementary indication for the current draw. Open the ASTROLOGICAL TABLE BALLANCHE. Distribute the 36 cards under the shape of this table, thus 12 rows of 3 cells each.

b) Analyze this draw of 36 cards at first sight (groups of cards possessing the same values, the cards upright and reversed, etc.). Then analyze the cards two by two, by decans. That means: the virtual card that is inscribed on Ballanche's table, with the real card, which is in front of the Inquirer, for the same location.

Example:
1) The row of the sign of Aries contains the cards 15, 21 and 24. The same line that we obtain after the distribution of cards is: 17, 6, and 25.
2) We analyze first the 36 cards, then the pairs, thus: 15 with 17, 21 with 6, and 24 with 25.
3) We obtain in this manner the events of three decans of the Aries.
4) If we execute this draw in the month of May, this line is situated in past.
5) If we execute the spread in January, this line will be found in the future. It should be remembered that the zodiacal signs (*Aries, Taurus*, etc.) do not have the same chronology as the months of the year (*March, April, May*, etc.), focusing thus to avoid the amalgam.
6) Also, take into account that the *Aries*, which is in the first House (House 1) is not associated with January, the first month of the year!

23. THE ASTROLOGICAL SPREAD OF 12 HOUSES
—*personal life's image*

This spread is a bit more complicated than the previous, but very rewarding, as it analyzes the life of the Inquirer according to the rules of the 12 Astrological Houses, from birth to the end.

Of course, it would be much better to have all astrological knowledge necessary for such a complex analysis but, in the meantime, one can always try to decipher the oracle! Remember that this is only a game. Don't take everything to heart or literally, but try to obtain from this analysis useful information about personal behavior. The divination games are a pleasant way of self-analysis. We can thus enjoy these moments of meditation, spent in personal companionship (and *faithful*), in trying to improve oneself and learn how to better control himself, by enjoying the personal reasoning capabilities, and by searching for new territories of inner development.

What is missing to the Petit Jeu (except the user's manual written by the hand of Pierre-Simon Ballanche) are the cards that could have designated the North and South Nodes, the Dark Moon or the Part of Fortune. We have not found a better idea than to introduce in their place four cards of another game. We note these cards with the missing astrological symbols and we mix them to the other ones if we wish to have ampler information on the draw. We note the personal ascendancy.

Let us enumerate the features provided by these positions in the chart, as set by astrologers:
- The position of the North Node represents the advantages needing to be reached and exploited.
- The position of the South Node represents the handicaps to overcome in life but also in oneself.
- The Part of Fortune helps to understand the personal values and the meaning that a human being gives to his life.
- The Black Moon does not have the same meaning for women and men, it will be necessary to consult books on astrology.

We remove out of the game the card that represents the ascendancy, and we put it in its place, in the first House. We place the cards in 12 rows, as in the ASTROLOGICAL TABLE BALLANCHE. We also put each of four added cards (mixed previously with the rest of 36 cards of the Petit Jeu) *on the card that they follow*, in the order of the pile. Of course, the Nodes will be situated at an interval of six Houses. Thus, when we find the first Node, we know where it will be necessary to put the second, as they have to be in perfect opposition. This way, we get important information, which can sometimes change the predictions.

We interpret the results by associating and analyzing the two cards that are at the same position, considering their sympathies or natural astrological oppositions with their neighboring.

For resuming the explanations in order:

a) We mix the cards face on the table, shuffle and cut. The cards are distributed in the order in which they disclose themselves, but we put the ascendant in the 1st House when it appears in the game.
b) When we arrive at one of the four new cards introduced in the game (remember that the Inquirer is not obliged at all to use them if this system does not suit him) this card is placed at the location of the card that preceded it. If this is one of the two lunar Nodes, place the first Node where it arrives, but the second must be put in the opposite of the first. (*Example*: if the South Node is in House 3, then the North Node is necessarily located in House 9.)
c) We make the interpretation according to the rules of the astrology, but we also take into account the meaning of the cards in the Petit Jeu. Do not forget the conjunctions, trigons, sextiles, etc.
d) We analyze the spread of 36 cards, and then the cards by pairs of two and by decans. That is to say: the virtual card that figures in the ASTROLOGICAL TABLE BALLANCHE with the real card that is in front of the Inquirer for the same location.

Example:

The line of Aries contains the cards 15, 21 and 24. The same line obtained by the Inquirer after spreading the cards is: 17, 6, and 25. We analyze the pairs, so: 15 with 17, 21 and 6, 24 and 25, by referring to their amity or their oppositions such as planets, but also like cards in the Petit Jeu.

24. THE CALCULATION OF TIME

1	2	3	4	5	6	7	8	9
1. Cavalier	2. Clover	3. Ship	4. House	5. Tree	6. Cloud	7. Snake	8. Coffin	9. Bouquet
10. Scythe	11. Rod	12. Birds	13. Child	14. Fox	15. Bear	16. Star	17. Stork	18. Dog
19. H. Tower	20. Garden	21. Mountain	22. Path	23. Mice	24. Heart	25. Ring	26. Book	27. Letter
28. Gentleman	29. Lady	30. Lily	31. Sun	32. Moon	33. Key	34. Fish	35. Anchor	36. Cross

The fact that Pierre-Simon Ballanche has assigned numbers to cards, in addition to their traditional values (Six, Seven, etc.) is due in no case to chance. By continuing the observations from a mathematical point of view, we see that each of the 36 cards can be reduced to a basic number. This operation is called *recursive reduction*.

By proceeding this way for the card 34, for example, we obtain: $3 + 4 = 7$. Similarly, for 29: $2 + 9 =$

11, which give us, by continuing the operation: 1 + 1 = 2.

This leads to the observation that all 36 cards in the game, except for the first row of the table below, can each be reduced to a more easily interpretable number, ranging from 1 to 9. This will be used to develop the method of calculation of time for the predictions.

Referring to the primary source, which is the game of Etteilla, by accumulating information and by developing his method, the present book introduces a singular measure instrument, which allows arranging the predictions in chronological order. According to Etteilla, by adding the numbers of the cards of a spread, we get the number of days, weeks, months or years (see *Etteilla's 12 cards spread*).

Etteilla had also used a particular method to divide the sum of days into months and weeks. In this spread, we add the numbers of twelve cards shown. According to the famous fortune teller of the 18th century, the result represents the number of days that close the past, present and future of the Inquirer (compared with the information on this specific draw). More specifically, information contained in this spread involves twice that number. First: the Inquirer's past for this number of days. Secondly: the future of the Inquirer for the same number of days. For example: the number 187 (obtained after adding together) represents 187 days for the past, but also 187 days for the future.

It should be recognized that few of us will be inclined to do spreads that refer to a future so distant. This is why we present below a method derived from that of Etteilla, but which is more convenient and adequate to the requirements of modern beings pressed that we are.

We take as an example a random draw for an Inquirer, and we arrange the cards from bottom to top and from left to right:

		35	21	25	18		
13	19	28	30	33	17	2	10
7	31	8	14	3	11	32	27
36	24	20	16	29	1	4	15
34	22	6	26	5	12	9	23

To make things easier for the readers who are using the Lady and the Gentleman as CP cards, we will agree that the Lady's card represents the woman-Inquirer. In our example, the card is on the second line from bottom upward. It is from the CP (Card of the Person, or Inquirer) that we always start to count.

- The first line from below, as well as the cards 36, 24, 20 and 16, is in the past, more or less close to the Inquirer.
- Cards that are to the right of the CP (1, 4, and 15) and all others (which are above, on the three remaining lines) are positioned in the future.

- To avoid mistakes, we will note positive (with the + sign) the cards of the future and negative (with the —sign) the cards from the past. As in arithmetic (and for not to confuse visually), we will just write the signs *minus*, the *plus* sign being, so, implied.
- We note on a sheet of paper the 36 cards in order. We start to make additions and recursive reductions for each card, starting from the CP. For the future, we start from the CP to the right, adding each card and then by writing the total on the list (each sum at its place on our list). Concerning the past, we start from CP towards the left.

1: 29+1 = 30 = 3+0 = **3** *(in the future)*
2: 29+1+4+15+7+31+8+14+3+11+32+27+13+19+28+30+ 33+17+2 = 324 = 3+2+4 = **9**
3: 29+1+4+15+7+31+8+14+3 = 112 = 1+1+2 = **4**
4: 34 = **7**
5: - 174 = **-3** *(in the past)*
6: -206 = **-8**
7: 56=11 = **2**
8: 95=14 = **5**
9: -157 = -13 = **-4**
10: 334=10 = **1**
11: 123= **6**
12: -169 = -16 = **-7**
13: 195=15 = **6**
14: 109=10 = **1**
15: 49=13 = **4**
16: -45 = **-9**

17 : 322= *7*
18 : 433=10 = *1*
19 : 214= *7*
20:-65 = -11 = *-2*
21 : 390=12 = *3*
22:-228 = -12 = *-3*
23:-148 = -13 = *-4*
24:-89 = -17 = *-8*
25 : 415=10 = *1*
26:-200 = *-2*
27 : 182=11 = *2*
28 : 242= *8*
29: CP
30 : 272=11 = *2*
31 : 87=15 = *6*
32 : 155=11 = *2*
33 : 305= *8*
34:-262 = -10 = *-1*
35 : 369=18 = *9*
36:-125 = *-8*

a) It is assumed that the draw is made on January 1st. We then note on the sheet of paper the date and we'll make portents for the days, weeks *or* months that follow this date.

b) It is necessary to decide before the draw for what period of time we wish the predictions (*either* days, *or* weeks, *or* months). The predictions begin one day after the date of the draw, because the CP is considered located in the present.

c) If you are only concerned about the future, negative numbers that are on the list of 36 cards are discarded. Otherwise, we analyze them in the same manner as the cards for the future, but by counting in the past.
d) Look now at our list of 36 cards. For each of them, we obtained (after addition and recursive reduction) a number from 1 to 9. The forecasts will therefore be for 9 days, 9 weeks *or* 9 months, as it was decided at the beginning.
e) We select the cards that have received the number **1** after the recursive reduction. These cards are 10, 14, 18 and 25, so Scythe, Fox, Dog and Ring. We note these cards following the order in which they appear in the draw, starting from the CP: 14, 10, 25 and 18. They will be the forecast cards for the day **+ 1**. So, if you count from the beginning of the year, it will be: January 1st + 1 = January the 2nd.
f) The procedure is the same for the cards that have received the number **2** after the recursive reduction. The cards obtained in the order of the draw are: 7, 32, 27, and 30. They will be the forecast cards for the day + 2, so January 1st + 2 = January 3rd.
g) We continue until we finish with the recursive reductions. According to the spread, we get this list for 9 days, 9 weeks *or* 9 months. The CP is situated in the current day, the future starts from tomorrow (so the present day + 1):

Day +1 *(January 2nd) or 1st week, or 1st month*: 14, 10, 25, 18
Day +2 *(January 3rd) or 2nd week, or 2nd month*: 7, 32, 27, 30
Day +3 *(January 4th) or 3rd week, or 3rd month*: 1, 21
Day +4 *(January 5th) or 4th week, or 4th month*: 15, 3
Day +5 *(January 6th) or 5th week, or 5th month*: 8
Day +6 *(January 7th) or 6th week, or 6th month*: 31, 11, 13
Day +7 *(January 8th) or 7th week, or 7th month*: 4, 19, 17
Day +8 *(January 9th) or 8th week, or 8th month*: 28, 33
Day +9 *(January 10th) or 9th week, or 9th month*: 2, 35.

The cards correspond to events situated on each of these dates. It may sometimes happen that you acquire a smaller number of cards, according to the spread. Or that we do not get cards for each day (or weeks, or months) on the 9 given in this example. We content ourselves in this case with the founded days, or another draw is made at another moment. If we obtain, for example, the CP in the last row, it is normal to have very little omens for the future, but enormously in the past.

THE PETIT JEU AND THE SIGNS OF THE ZODIAC

N°	THE CARD	SIGN OF THE ZODIAC	PERIOD (French system)	Decan	INTERVAL
1	CAVALIER	Cancer	June 21 — July 22	2	July 2 — July 12
2	CLOVER	Gemini	May 21 — June 20	1	May 21 — May 31
3	SHIP	Sagittarius	Nov 22 — December 20	2	December 2 — December 11
4	HOUSE	Taurus	April 21 — May 20	2	May 1 — May 11
5	TREE	Aquarius	January 20 — February 18	2	January 31 — February 8
6	CLOUD	Libra	September 23 — October 22	3	October 14 — October 22
7	SNAKE	Scorpio	October 23 — November 21	3	Nov 12 — November 21
8	COFFIN	Pisces	February 19 — March 20	3	March 10 — March 20
9	BOUQUET	Cancer	June 21 — July 22	1	June 22 — July 1
10	SCYTHE	Scorpio	October 23 — November 21	1	October 23 — November 2
11	ROD	Leo	July 23 — August 22	1	July 23 — August 2
12	BIRDS	Gemini	May 21 — June 20	2	June 1 — June 10

N°	THE CARD	SIGN OF THE ZODIAC	PERIOD (French system)	Decan	INTERVAL
13	CHILD	Virgo	August 23 – September 22	3	Sep 14 – September 22
14	FOX	Scorpio	October 23 – November 21	2	Nov 3 – November 11
15	BEAR	Aries	March 21 – April 20	1	March 21 – March 31
16	STAR	Pisces	February 19 – March 20	1	February 19 – February 29
17	STORK	Gemini	May 21 – June 20	3	June 11 – June 20
18	DOG	Libra	September 23 – October 22	1	September 23 – October 2
19	H. TOWER	Capricorn	December 21 – January 19	1	Dec 21 – December 31
20	GARDEN	Cancer	June 21 – July 22	3	July 13 – July 22
21	MOUNTAIN	Aries	March 21 – April 20	2	April 1 – April 11
22	PATH	Libra	September 23 – October 22	2	October 3 – October 13
23	MICE	Capricorn	December 21 – January 19	2	January 1 – January 9
24	HEART	Aries	March 21 – April 20	3	April 12 – April 20
25	RING	Leo	July 23 – August 22	2	August 3 – August 12

N°	THE CARD	SIGN OF THE ZODIAC	PERIOD (French system)	Decan	INTERVAL
26	BOOK	Sagittarius	Nov 22 — December 20	3	Dec 12 — December 20
27	LETTER	Aquarius	January 20 — February 18	1	January 20 — January 30
28	GENTLEMAN	Leo	July 23 — August 22	3	August 13 — August 22
29	LADY	Virgo	August 23 — September 22	2	Sep 2 — September 13
30	LILY	Taurus	April 21 — May 20	1	April 21 — April 30
31	SUN	Capricorn	December 21 — January 19	3	January 10 — January 19
32	MOON	Aquarius	January 20 — February 18	3	February 9 — February 18
33	KEY	Virgo	August 23 — September 22	1	August 23 — September 1
34	FISH	Sagittarius	Nov 22 — December 20	1	Nov 22 — December 1
35	ANCHOR	Taurus	April 21 — May 20	3	May 12 — May 20
36	CROSS	Pisces	February 19 — March 20	2	March 1 — March 9

TABLE OF CONTENTS :

SPREADS 11

  I. CLASSICAL SPREADS: 17

    1. THE 3 CARDS SPREAD 19

    2. THE 5 CARDS SPREAD 19

    3. THE 9 CARDS SPREAD 20

    4. THE GYPSY SPREAD OF 21 CARDS 21

    5. THE HORSESHOE SPREAD OF 21 CARDS 21

    6. THE SPREAD OF "YES AND NO" QUESTIONS 23

  II. ETTEILLA AND LENORMAND SPREAD: 25

    7. ETTEILLA'S 12 CARDS SPREAD 27

    8. THE 15 CARDS SPREAD 30

    9. THE 25 CARDS SPREAD 33

  III. SPREADS DERIVED FROM LENORMAND DISPOSITION: 41

    10. THE GRAND TABLEAU 41

    11. THE MOREAU SPREAD 43

    12. THE SPREAD IN THREE DIMENSIONS 47

  IV. NEW SPREADS: 49

    13. THE ENCOUNTER QUESTIONS' SPREAD 49

    14. THE PYRAMIDAL SPREAD 51

15. THE DIAMOND SPREAD	....	52
16. THE SMALL LOOP SPREAD	....	54
17. THE BIG LOOP SPREAD	....	56
18. THE GREAT PYRAMID SPREAD	....	59
19. THE HEART'S SPREAD	....	61
20. THE SPREAD IN Z	....	65
21. THE CROSS OF TIME	....	69
22. THE ASTROLOGICAL SPREAD	....	72
23. THE ASTROLOGICAL SPREAD OF 12 HOUSES	....	74
24. THE CALCULATION OF TIME	....	77
THE PETIT JEU AND THE SIGNS OF THE ZODIAC	....	85
TABLE OF CONTENTS	....	89

Impression numérique par :

www.amazon.com

Tirage achevé: janvier 2019

Dépôt légal BNF: janvier 2019, France

ISBN 979-10-94605-13-4

Printed in Great Britain
by Amazon